RACING AGAINST THE ODDS

The Story of Wendell Scott, Stock Car Racing's African-American Champion

by **Carole Boston Weatherford**   illustrated by **Eric A. Velasquez**

two lions

two lions

Amazon Publishing
Attn: Amazon Children's Publishing
P.O. Box 400818
Las Vegas, NV 89140
www.amazon.com/amazonchildrenspublishing

Library of Congress Cataloging-in-Publication Data

Weatherford, Carole Boston, 1956-
Racing against the odds: The story of Wendell Scott, stock car racing's African-American champion / by Carole Boston Weatherford;
illustrated by Eric Velasquez.
p. cm.
ISBN 978-1-4778-1093-4
1. Scott, Wendell—Juvenile literature 2. Stock car drivers—United States—Biography—Juvenile literature.
3. Automobile racing drivers—United States—Biography—Juvenile literature. 4. African American automobile racing drivers—
Biography—Juvenile literature. I. Velasquez, Eric, ill. II. Title. —
GV1032.S36W43 2008
796.72092—dc22
[B]
2008010711

The illustrations are rendered using Prismacolor Nupastels and Unison soft pastels on Wallis paper.
Book design by Daniel Roode
Editor: Margery Cuyler

To everyone who has ever chased a dream.
—C.B.W.

For my friends, Eric and Julie-Ann
—E.V.

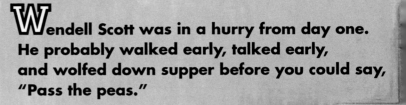

Wendell Scott was in a hurry from day one. He probably walked early, talked early, and wolfed down supper before you could say, "Pass the peas."

When his buddies were skating, playing tag, and pitching horseshoes, Scott was driving his mama to the grocery store in the family car— long before he was old enough to get a license.

At fourteen, he bought his first car—a Ford Model T— for fifteen bucks. In no time flat, he tore that clunker apart and rebuilt it good as new. Then, he quit school and drove a cab to put his sister through college.

Weekends, Scott and a friend went
to stock-car races; cheered from the stands.
"Would you have the nerve to race?" the friend
asked out of the blue. "Shucks, yeah," said Scott.

Burning rubber in that cab, Scott made
a name for himself—with the police.
Piled up umpteen speeding tickets
before he marched off to war.

After World War II, those tickets and fines were waiting for him. That put the brakes on taxi driving. Scott opened a garage, married, settled down, and started a family.

To make ends meet, he ran moonshine—
bootleg whiskey. Outran every deputy in the county.
So when a race promoter wanted a black driver,
the police said, "Scott's your man. Ain't nobody faster."

That race promoter asked Scott to hit the track,
and he didn't think twice about saying yes.
Before you could say, "Start your engines!"
Scott had souped up a 1939 Ford with junkyard parts.

At the dirt track that day in 1947, white drivers pulled names from a hat to see who would run him off the track. A record crowd watched his Ford fall to pieces before the last lap. But Scott was hooked.

He meant to race all over the South. Some tracks turned him away, but he came back till they ran out of excuses and let him race. Then, he gave them a run for their money.

Some white drivers played dirty, banged up Scott's car so bad that he carried spare parts. But a few drivers lent a hand. Once, Scott's truck broke down, stranding him on the highway. Another driver towed him to the next track.

Racing was a family affair; Scott's sons on the pit crew, his daughters keeping score, and his wife Mary driving the racecar hauler and serving soul food from the truck. With his own cheering section, Scott could ignore the jeers.

By 1961, with a hundred-some wins on the Dixie Outlaw Circuit, Scott was ready to move up to Grand National races. But how—with hand-me-down cars, a hauler converted from an old tire truck, and no big-money backers?

Lap by lap, that's how; scrimping, scrounging, sacrificing, never forgetting he had six mouths to feed; one pocket nearly broke, the other pocket full of dreams. Scott revved his engine, floored the gas pedal, and ripped around the curves.

In 1962, when his car turned on its side, he crawled out,
tipped it back on its wheels, and drove thirty more laps
with gravel slashing his face through the shattered windshield.
He stopped only because his sons begged him to.

In the summer of 1963, Scott's Chevy was running like a charm.
At Speedway Park, Jacksonville, Florida, he sped ahead
and stayed out front. But when he crossed the finish line,
no checkered flag, no "Wendell Scott wins!" on the loudspeaker.

Then, the flag went down—for Buck Baker, not for Scott. The judges claimed Scott was third. Baker spun into the winner's circle, got a trophy and a kiss from a beauty queen. But the race was not over for Scott. He pressed the judges. Two hours later, they ruled him the winner.

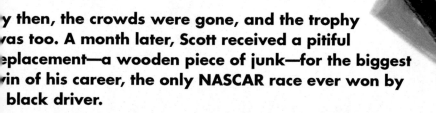

y then, the crowds were gone, and the trophy
vas too. A month later, Scott received a pitiful
eplacement—a wooden piece of junk—for the biggest
vin of his career, the only NASCAR race ever won by
black driver.

Still an underdog, Scott kept racing—ten more years, repairing his own car, painting "Mechanic Me" on the body, putting together entrance fees dollar by dollar, careful not to blow an engine, and finishing in the top ten year after year.

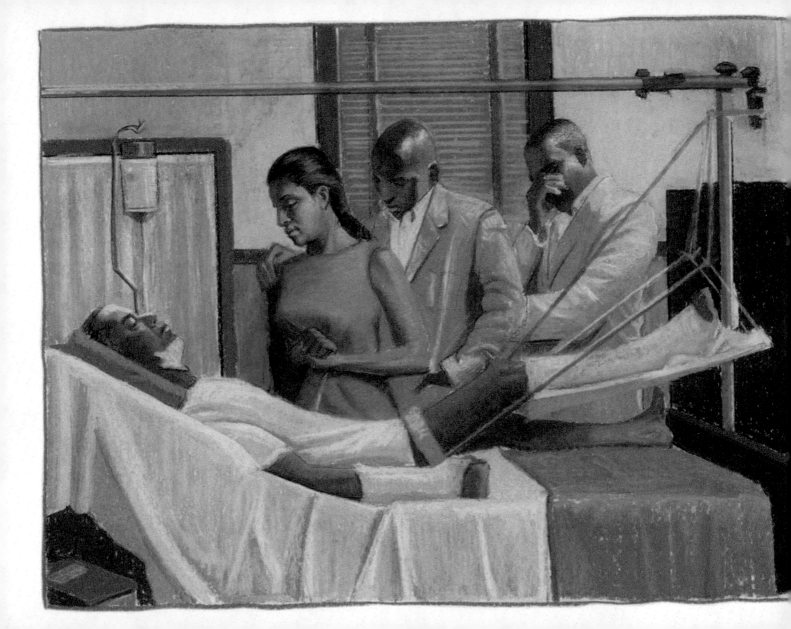

Though strapped for cash, Scott never considered quitting.
Never. It took a crash to slow him down—
a twenty-one-car, 180-mile-per-hour smashup that crushed his
car
and more bones than he could count.

Four months out of the hospital, Scott gave racing
one more shot, drove his last lap in the big leagues,
then parked his wrecked Mercury Cyclone behind the garage
and let rust claim it while he fixed customers' cars.

Between racing and his garage, Scott put all his children through college. And when Hollywood made a movie about his life, he built three cars for the film and even drove in action scenes. *Greased Lightning*. Yessiree!

For him, racing was never about money or skin color.
He loved to turn the wheel of a racecar, work magic on an engine,
and then push it faster than it was ever meant to go.
Racing pumped through his veins like fuel in a carburetor.

Scott didn't just dust the competition, he blazed a trail.

A Note from the Author

Wendell O. Scott was NASCAR's first and most successful African-American driver. Born in 1921 in Danville, Virginia, he bought his first car, a Ford Model T, for $15, at age fourteen. A former cab driver, World War II veteran, and self-taught mechanic, Scott opened a garage after the war. Like many early NASCAR drivers, he got his start hauling bootleg liquor, known as moonshine, to towns where liquor sales were outlawed. Scott drove so fast that the police never caught him. But they did pass his name along to a racetrack promoter who was looking for a fast black driver.

Scott, who owned a garage and began racing in 1947, faced a hard road during the segregation era. Racetracks tried to bar him, and some drivers banged up his car to run him out of the sport. Scott persevered, though, winning 120 races in the sport's lower divisions before moving up to the Grand National division. His wife and children traveled with him from race to race.

Scott competed in more than five hundred races in NASCAR's top division from 1961 through the early 1970s. Although he never had a new car or a major sponsor, he finished in the top ten 147 times and in 1966 finished sixth in the standings. His only Grand National win came at Jacksonville, Florida, in 1963. He is the first and only black driver ever to win a NASCAR race.

In 1973, Scott retired from racing. He was still manning his garage when the 1977 film *Greased Lightning* depicted his life. Scott died in 1990. In 1997, the street where he once lived was renamed Wendell Scott Drive. In 1999, he was inducted into the International Motorsports Hall of Fame in Talladega, Alabama.

CAROLE BOSTON WEATHERFORD has written more than twenty children's books, many of them on African-American themes. Her recent picture-book biographies include *I, Matthew Henson: Polar Explorer* and *Jesse Owens: Fastest Man Alive*, both illustrated by Eric Velasquez. In addition, she is the author of *Moses: When Harriet Tubman Led Her People to Freedom*, a Caldecott Honor award winner. Her other titles include *The Sound That Jazz Makes*, an NAACP Image Award finalist and winner of the Carter G. Woodson Award from the National Council for the Social Studies and *Remember the Bridge: Poems of a People*, winner of the Juvenile Literature Award from the American Association of University Women, North Carolina. A college literature professor and mother of two sons, she lives in High Point, North Carolina. To find out more about the author, visit her at www.caroleweatherford.com.

ERIC A. VELASQUEZ was born in Spanish Harlem and grew up in Harlem. He attended the High School of Art and Design and earned his BFA from the School of Visual Arts. He was awarded the Coretta Scott King/John Steptoe Award for New Talent for his first picture book, *The Piano Man*, by Debbi Chocolate. He has illustrated many books since then, including *The Rain Stomper* by Addie Boswell and *Grandma's Records*, a story he wrote and illustrated. He lives and works in Hartsdale, New York. To find out more about the illustrator, visit him at www.ericvelasquez.com.

Made in the USA
Monee, IL
19 August 2023